For Benny
from Uncle Paul
Christmas 2010.

Growing Up a Country Boy

Life Is Best When You're Barefoot and Carefree

Paintings by
Donald Zolan

HARVEST HOUSE PUBLISHERS

EUGENE, OREGON

Growing Up a Country Boy

Artwork by Donald Zolan
Text copyright © 2004 by Harvest House Publishers
Eugene, Oregon 97402
www.harvesthousepublishers.com

ISBN 0-7369-1190-1

John Deere® is a registered trademark and appears in this book with the permission of Deere and Company, Moline, Illinois.

Design and production by Garborg Design Works, Minneapolis, Minnesota

Harvest House Publishers has made every effort to trace the ownership of all poems and quotes. In the event of a question arising from the use of a poem or quote, we regret any error made and will be pleased to make the necessary correction in future editions of this book.

Select stanzas of "Boyhood Memories" by Howard B. Austin are used by permission of the Austin family.

Scripture quotations are taken from *The Living Bible,* Copyright © 1971. Used by permission of Tyndale House Publishers, Inc., Wheaton, IL 60189 USA. All rights reserved.

Printed in Hong Kong

05 06 07 08 09 10 / NG / 10 9 8 7 6 5

One is given
many chances
to be a man;
one can be
a boy but once.

EMERY POTTLE

Already a dozen boys had donned old clothes and were somersaulting and tumbling and romping about on the snow-covered lawn, unconsciously working off some of that inexhaustible store of energy that seems to increase miraculously in the very act of being consumed. Yes, they were good boys, thought Mr. Hyde; terribly youthful, of course, and inexperienced, but that was inevitable. It wasn't fair to blame them for what they couldn't help...Boys were boys.

H.C. KITTREDGE
"The Undiscovered Country"
Atlantic Monthly, 1920

Christopher Robin was sitting outside his door, putting on his Big Boots. As soon as he saw the Big Boots, Pooh knew that an Adventure was going to happen, and he brushed the honey off his nose with the back of his paw, and spruced himself up as well as he could, so as to look Ready for Anything.

A. A. MILNE
Winnie-the-Pooh

The silver lining was the euphoria at my release once the service ended as I ran home clawing at the necktie for relief and extracting myself from the bondage of the suit jacket. Ah, jeans, sneakers and a flannel shirt. Onto my bike and up to the farm and the warmth of the cows in the barn and the tease of spring in Vermont as nature spoke to me with a connection of spirit. God knew the needs of young boys on Easter afternoons.

LYMAN ORTON

I still find each day too short for all the thoughts I want to think, all the walks I want to take, all the books I want to read and all the friends I want to see.

JOHN BURROUGHS

Farmer Brown's boy kept on his way, laughing at the fright of old Jed Thumper. Presently he reached the springs from which came the water that made the very beginning of the Laughing Brook. He expected to find them dry, for way down on the Green Meadows the Smiling Pool was nearly dry, and the Laughing Brook was nearly dry, and he had supposed that of course the reason was that the springs where the Laughing Brook started were no longer bubbling.

But they were! The clear cold water came bubbling up out of the ground just as it always had, and ran off down into the Green Forest in a little stream that would grow and grow as it ran and became the Laughing Brook. Farmer Brown's boy took off his ragged old straw hat and scowled down at the bubbling water just as if it had no business to be bubbling there.

Of course, he didn't think just that. The fact is, he didn't know just what he did think. Here were the springs bubbling away just as they always had. There was the little stream starting off down into the Green Forest with a gurgle that by and by would become a laugh, just as it always had. And yet down on the Green Meadows on the other side of the Green Forest there was no longer a Laughing Brook or a Smiling Pool. He felt as if he ought to pinch himself to make sure that he was awake and not dreaming.

THORNTON W. BURGESS
The Adventures of Paddy the Beaver

It was one of those sparkling winter nights when a boy feels that though the world is very big, he himself is bigger; that under the whole crystalline blue sky there is no one quite so warm and sentient as himself, and that all this magnificence is for him.

WILLA CATHER
One of Ours

What we have a right to expect of the American boy is that he shall turn out to be a good American man. The boy can best become a good man by being a good boy—not a goody-goody boy, but just a plain good boy..."Good," in the largest sense, should include whatever is fine, straightforward, clean, and manly.

THEODORE ROOSEVELT

The boys dressed themselves, hid their accoutrements, and went off grieving that there were no outlaws any more, and wondering what modern civilization could claim to have done to compensate for their loss. They said they would rather be outlaws a year in Sherwood Forest than President of the United States forever.

MARK TWAIN
The Adventures of Tom Sawyer

11

Boys are found everywhere—on top of, underneath, inside of, climbing on, swinging from, running around or jumping to. Mothers love them, little girls hate them, older sisters and brothers tolerate them, adults ignore them and Heaven protects them. A boy is Truth with dirt on its face, Beauty with a cut on its finger, Wisdom with bubble gum in its hair and the Hope of the future with a frog in its pocket.

ALAN BECK

The boy listened to the wind passing through the tops of the tall pines; he thought they moved like giant brooms sweeping the sky. The moonlight raced down through the broken spaces of swaying trees and sent bright shafts of light along the ground and over him. The voice of the wind in the pines reminded him of one of the stories his mother had told him about King David. The Lord had said to David that when he heard the wind moving in the tops of the cedar trees, he would know that the Lord was fighting on his side and he would win...

The boy listened to the wind. He could hear the mighty roaring. He thought he heard the voice of David and the tramping of many feet. He wasn't afraid with David near. He thought he saw a lantern moving far off in the woods, and as he fell asleep he thought he heard the deep, ringing voice of Sounder rising out of his great throat, riding the mist of the lowlands.

WILLIAM ARMSTRONG
Sounder

The trail of the Boy was always distinct, but on this especial morning it lay over house, porch, barn—everything. The Mother followed it up, stooping to gather the miscellany of toying belongings into her apron. She had a delightful scheme in her mind for clearing everything up. She wanted to see how it would seem, for once, not to have any litter of whittlings, of strings and marbles, and tops! No litter of beloved birds' eggs, snake-skins, turtleshells!

ANNE HAMILTON DOUNELL
"The Boy"
Harper's Monthly Magazine, 1901

Sodden, and with his nose slightly enlarged upon one side, Harvey retired to his own quarters, and, desiring to avoid his mother, went upstairs to the attic, and thence through a scuttle to a more interesting place, the roof of the house. Here he partly dried himself in the sun, and then, observing that he had the attention of several children in the yard next door, he began to perform hazardous feats of climbing. Twice he risked his life and once probably would have lost it, except for the fact that as he slipped downward to the abyss his toe caught by chance in a copper rain-gutter. He murmured "Whee!" and then waved his hand with boastful grace, to show his admirers below that the thing had been done precisely as intended.

BOOTH TARKINGTON
"What I Have Learned from Boys"
American Magazine, 1925

But fate is sometimes kind even to those who deserve its hardest kicks, and just as the outlook seemed absolutely hopeless there came a cry of joy which no language can describe, which no rhapsody can express—the clear, glad exultation of the boy who had just caught his first fish.

Gone were all the disappointments, forgotten were all cares, forgiven were all wrongs—there was the fish squirming and dangling at the end of the line and he had caught it—caught it himself without anybody's help!

LYNN ROBY MEEKINGS
"A Boy Goes Fishing"
The Outing Magazine, 1901

I squatted on this bank and dropped in my line. I did so want to catch a fish. One fish would set me upon my way, because I had read how much you can learn from one fish…The grub went down to the bottom of the stream. It swirled around and hung still. Suddenly the string came to life, and rode back and forth and around in a circle. I pulled with a powerful jerk. The hook came apart and whatever I had went circling back to its bed…I whittled another hook, but this time I cheated and used string to wind it together instead of bark. I walked back to the log and luckily found another grub. I hurried to the pool, and I flipped a trout out of the water before I knew I had a bite.

JEAN GEORGE
My Side of the Mountain

For the period of boyhood is one distinct and separate from two others, the whole of those years up to Manhood being divided into three parts. First, there is the stage of Childhood up to, say, the twelfth year. Secondly, there is the stage of real Boyhood, up to the sixteenth or eighteenth year, when he leaves home for work or college. Thirdly, there is that period wherein he is a Youth, a period in turn bounded on its last extremity by his twenty-first year, in which he reaches Manhood.

STEPHEN M. DALE
"Memories of an Early Boyhood"
The Independent, 1904

Never before had Pete felt so strong, so fast, so terrifically happy! As he raced over the wet grass, he felt he could fly if he wanted to; take right off and bring back the orange-juice sun for breakfast! Then his feet were pounding over the weather-beaten boards of the diving platform and he did fly! SPLASH! *The freezing water became a screaming, churning mass of legs and arms and backs. Then they were out again, racing back up the slope.*

A few moments later, Pete was prancing around the cabin floor with the other Mohicans, rubbing his goose-bumped skin with a big, fluffy towel. Oh! the joy of it! The pure, laughing, sunshiny, dew-grassed joy of it!

RODERICK HUFF
Bugle Boy

Before I was five, I helped with the little activities of the domestic service. My mother and father were devoted Christians. My father asked the blessing of Heaven at every meal. When the work of the day was done and bedtime came, we gathered around the fireplace in winter. We each took part in reading a chapter from the New Testament. Then we all kneeled down and father made the evening prayer. The younger children, and I was next to the youngest, went to bed with perfect confidence that the dawn would awaken us safe and happy. The memory of these prayers is the most delightful of all my recollections of childhood.

Dr. Harvey W. Wiley

We raced through the crisp November woods, kicking brown leaves into the air with a dry rustle that crackled with its own happiness. As we scampered through the autumn forest, the sound that we earlier had heard was now smothered.

We stopped.

"Hear it?" said a breathless Soup.

"Now it's louder."

"We must be getting closer. Let's go."

Again we ran, until Wicker's Woods ended in a rail fence. Soup vaulted over and I was fast on his heels. We were in an open field. We'd never been this far before on any of our Saturday morning hikes. Our feet jumped across row after row of corn stubble...Now that we were in the open instead of traveling through fallen leaves, I could hear the noise even as we ran.

Robert Newton Peck
Soup & Me

Downstairs for a dab at your face in the wash basin—and cold it felt, too. Then into your stiff boots which had been left overnight to dry behind the kitchen stove. Father's tracks were far apart and deep on the way to the barn, but you took the stride like a man. Once there, in the close, musty, hay-smelling atmosphere, you hurried through the "chores," pulling down fodder for horses and cattle in desperation of haste, for you were eager to be off to the upper lot to set "figure four" traps for rabbits before breakfast.

Theoretically it was strictly required of boys to come home after school—"straight." This was something that could be evaded with elastic resource...If the sun had softened the snow during the day there was always a snowball fight to the death between the Hill and the Hollow.

Halfway down the slope stood a gigantic pine, long a landmark of the section; here the road accomplished a hair-raising curve. The more timorous souls started at this point to make the coast but the hardier spirits dragged their bobs clean up to the top, where stood the cemetery in chilly warning and with a whoop flung themselves down on their sleds and were off. It was the proudest day of my boy time when singly and alone I could steer my bob from the top of the hill down, taking the pine-tree curve in all the arrogance of a sure hand and terrific speed, safely avoid the worst "bumps" and the town pump, and bring up, panting and watery-eyed, a mile away.

EMERY POTTLE
"Memories of a Boy-Time Winter"
The Outing Magazine, 1903

By the little wrinkles that bunched up on her forehead, I could tell that Mama wasn't satisfied. Papa came in during one of these inspections. Mama told him she was worried about my health.

"Aw," he said, "there's nothing wrong with him. It's just because he's been cooped up all winter. A boy needs sunshine, and exercise. He's almost eleven now, and I'm going to let him help me in the fields this summer. That will put the muscles back on him."

I thought this was wonderful. I'd finally grown up to be a man. I was going to help Papa with the farm.

WILSON RAWLS
Where the Red Fern Grows

The ache turned into a longing for the fawn. He got up and brought a handful of peanuts for the 'coon, to keep it occupied. He went in search of the fawn. He found it behind a myrtle bush, where it had been able to watch unobserved. He thought it might be thirsty, too, and he offered it water in the bear cub's pan. The fawn sniffed and would not drink…He sat down under a live oak and held the fawn close to him. There was a comfort in it not to be found in the hairy arms of Buck Forrester. He wondered if his pleasure in Fodder-wing's creatures had been dissipated because Fodder-wing was gone, or because the fawn now held all he needed of delight.

He said to it, "I'd not trade you for all of 'em, and the cub to boot."

A gratifying feeling of faithfulness came over him, that the enchantment of the creatures he had so coveted could not deflect his affections from the fawn.

MARJORIE KINNAN RAWLINGS
The Yearling

25

oger turned and looked back. He had passed the butternut tree. He had walked right through the deep hole from end to end. He could go back and do it again. He could do it a hundred times, a million times, and it would be just the same.

A great shadow had been lifted suddenly off the world, letting in again all the sunlight, all the color. There was nothing left to be afraid of anymore, ever. He wanted to shout, to jump.

As he ran splashing through the shallows, kicking the water to right and left, he looked up and saw Rob, there on the bank watching him.

Rob smiled, leaning on his hay rake. He said, "Got all wet, didn't you?"

"Uh-huh!" said Roger.

"Sort of slipped in, I suppose?"

"Uh-huh."

"I saw you."

Roger waited a moment wriggling his toes in the grass. But Rob said nothing more. He just stood there, smiling. The sun shone on the clean, cropped hayfield, the glad bushes, the woods and the hills beyond them stretching up to the blue sky. The whole world was glorious, dazzling. And the sound of the brook was like a chorus of little friendly voices all singing together.

Roger caught sight of the laden hay wagon, already far away, creaking on its last trip to the barn. He gave a sudden bound and leaping, shouting, waving his arms above his head, he began to gallop like a little crazy goat across the pasture and up the slope to the lane.

MARGERY BIANCO
"Boy in the Brook"
Good Housekeeping, 1928

They worked fast, pitching hay into the mangers below. Almanzo could hear the crunching of all the animals eating. The haymows were warm with the warmth of all the stock below, and the hay smelled dusty-sweet. There was a smell, too, of the horses and cows, and a wooly smell of sheep. And before the boys finished filling the mangers there was the good smell of warm milk foaming into Father's pail.

LAURA INGALLS WILDER
Farmer Boy

After that there was nothing to do but sit still till the sermon was over. It was two hours long. Almanzo's legs ached and his jaw wanted to yawn, but he dared not yawn or fidget. He must sit perfectly still and never take his eyes from the preacher's solemn face and wagging beard. Almanzo couldn't understand how Father knew that he wasn't looking at the preacher, if Father was looking at the preacher himself. But Father always did know.

At last it was over. In the sunshine outside the church, Almanzo felt better.

LAURA INGALLS WILDER
Farmer Boy

The next day was a busy one for me. With the hampering help of my sisters I made the little doghouse. Papa cut the ends off his check lines and gave them to me for collars. With painstaking care, deep in the tough leather I scratched the name "Old Dan" on one and "Little Ann" on the other. With a nail and a rock two holes were punched in each of the straps. I put them around their small necks and laced the ends together with bailing wire.

That evening I had a talk with my mother. I told her about praying for the two pups, about the magazine and the plans I had made. I told her how hard I had tried to find names for them and how strange it was finding them carved in the bark of a sycamore tree.

With a smile on her face, she asked, "Do you believe God heard your prayer and helped you?"

"Yes, Mama," I said. "I know He did and I'll always be thankful."

Wilson Rawls
Where the Red Fern Grows

It was wonderful indeed how I could have heart-to-heart talks with my dogs and they always seemed to understand. Each question I asked was answered in their own doggish way. Although they couldn't talk in my terms, they had a language of their own that was easy to understand. Sometimes I would see the answer in their eyes, and again it would be in the friendly wagging of their tails. Other times I could hear the answer in a low whine or feel it in the soft caress of a warm flicking tongue. In some way, they would always answer.

Wilson Rawls
Where the Red Fern Grows

Rest is not idleness, and to lie sometimes on the grass under trees on a summer's day, listening to the murmur of the water, or watching the clouds float across the sky, is by no means a waste of time.

J. LUBBOCK

Joe Carraclough had never expected to see Lassie any more...But somewhere, down far in the depths of his hopes, he had dreamed of it, without ever believing his dream would come true. And when he came from school that day and saw Lassie waiting, exactly as usual, he felt that it was not true—he was only living in his dreams. He stared at the dog, his broad, boyish face full of amazement.

ERIC KNIGHT
Lassie Come Home

Since he had started playing with his father's hound puppies a great dream had grown within him. Some day he would find a dog to shame all others, a fine dog that he could treasure, and cherish, and breed from so that all who loved fine dogs would come to see and buy his. That would be all he wanted of Heaven.

JIM KJELGAARD
Big Red

"I reckon I ain't dressed fitten for a pirate," said he, with a regretful pathos in his voice; "but I ain't got none but these."

But the other boys told him the fine clothes would come fast enough, after they should have begun their adventures...Gradually their talk died out and drowsiness began to steal upon the eyelids of the little waifs. The pipe dropped from the fingers of the Red-handed, and he slept the sleep of the conscience-free and the weary.

MARK TWAIN
The Adventures of Tom Sawyer

He was that glad to see me again he didn't know what to do. And he wanted to know all about it right off; because it was a grand adventure, and mysterious, and so it hit him where he lived.

MARK TWAIN
The Adventures of Huckleberry Finn

35

Teach a child to choose the right path, and when he is olde

Foot-races followed, and, burning to distinguish himself also, Jack insisted on trying, though his mother warned him that the weak leg might be harmed, and he had his own doubts about it, as he was all out of practice. However, he took his place with a handkerchief tied round his head, red shirt and stockings, and his sleeves rolled up as if he meant business. Jill and Molly could not sit still during this race, and stood on the bank quite trembling with excitement as the half-dozen runners stood in a line at the starting-post waiting for the word "Go!"

Off they went at last over the smooth beach to the pole with the flag at the further end, and everyone watched them with mingled interest and merriment, for they were a droll set, and the running not at

he will remain upon it.

THE BOOK OF PROVERBS

all scientific with most of them. One young fisherman with big boots over his trousers started off at a great pace, pounding along in the most dogged way, while a little chap in a tight bathing-suit with very thin legs skimmed by him, looking so like a sand-piper it was impossible to help laughing at both. Jack's former training stood him in good stead now; for he went to work in professional style, and kept a steady trot till the flagpole had been passed, then he put on his speed and shot ahead of all the rest, several of whom broke down and gave up. But Cox and Bacon held on gallantly; and soon it was evident that the sturdy legs in the knickerbockers were gaining fast, for Jack gave his ankle an ugly wrench on a round pebble, and the weak knee began to fail. He did his best, however, and quite a breeze of enthusiasm stirred the spectators as the three boys came down the course like mettlesome horses, panting, pale, or purple, but each bound to win at any cost.

LOUISA MAY ALCOTT
Jack and Jill

It was nearly noon the following day when Shasta was wakened by something warm and soft moving over his face. He opened his eyes and found himself staring into the long face of a horse; its nose and lips were almost touching his. He remembered the exciting events of the previous night and sat up...But the horse nuzzled at him with its nose and pawed him gently with a hoof till he had to get up. And then he looked about him and saw where they were. Behind them lay a little copse. Before them the turf, dotted with white flowers, sloped down to the brow of a cliff. Far below them so that the sound of the breaking waves was very faint, lay the sea.

C.S. LEWIS *The Horse and His Boy*

You are worried about seeing him spend his early years in doing nothing. What! Is it nothing to be happy? Nothing to skip, play, and run around all day long? Never in his life will he be so busy again.

JEAN-JACQUES ROUSSEAU

Mrs. Darling came to the window, for at present she was keeping a sharp eye on Wendy. She told Peter that she had adopted all the other boys, and would like to adopt him also.

"Would you send me to school?" he inquired craftily.

"Yes."

"And then to an office?"

"I suppose so."

"Soon I would be a man?"

"Very soon."

"I don't want to go to school and learn solemn things," he told her passionately. "I don't want to be a man...Keep back, lady, no one is going to catch me and make me a man."

J.M. BARRIE *Peter Pan*

Whether sixty or sixteen, there is in every human being's heart the love of wonder, the sweet amazement at the stars and the starlike things, the undaunted challenge of events, the unfailing childlike appetite for what-next, and the joy of the game of living.

SAMUEL ULLMAN

Look without!
Behold the beauty of the day,
The shout
Of color to glad color,
Rocks and trees,
And sun and seas,
And wind and sky:
All these
Are God's expression,
Art work of His hand,
Which men must love
Ere they can understand.

RICHARD HOVEY

Hitch your wagon to a star.

RALPH WALDO EMERSON

Be the Best Wherever You Are!

If you can't be a pine on the top of the hill,
  Be a scrub in the valley—but be
The best little scrub by the side of the rill;
  Be a bush if you can't be a tree.

If you can't be a bush, be a bit of the grass,
  Some highway happier make;
If you can't be a muskie, then just be a bass—
  But the liveliest bass in the lake!

We can't all be captains, we've got to be crew,
  There's something for all of us here,
There's big work to do, and there's lesser to do,
  And the task we must do is the near.

If you can't be a highway, then just be a trail,
  If you can't be the sun, be a star;
It isn't by size that you win or you fail—
  Be the best of whatever you are!

DOUGLAS MALLOCH

*Little Samuel was growing in
two ways—he was getting taller
and he was becoming everyone's
favorite (and he was a favorite
of the Lord's too!)*

THE BOOK OF 1 SAMUEL

43

Father had been plowing way over across the tracks, and I didn't think he'd noticed us, because he never stopped to look when I could see him. I ran out to meet him when he came, and got all mixed up, I was trying to tell him so fast. He put his hand out and rumpled up my hair. I didn't know what he meant, but he said, "I guess you're a chip off the old chopping block..." We walked along a little way, then he rumpled my hair again and said, "Your father was proud of you, Son." It was the first time he ever told me that, and I got a lump in my throat.

RALPH MOODY
Little Britches

After a boy's chores were done of a morning, the woodbox filled for the day, the stable cleaned, the chickens fed, the cow picketed, the horse curried, the boy was his own master.

WILLIAM ALLEN WHITE
"Boys—Then and Now"
American Magazine, 1926

Boyhood Memories

Just at the turn of the century,
My mem'ry takes me back
To times long gone when a bare-foot boy
In truth did nothing lack.
A little farm in Illinois
Was the stage beyond compare,
Where as a lad I lived and grew
And found that life was fair.

Just forty acres rolling land
Near a lazy, muddy creek,
That knew the stirrings of the spring
And winters cold and bleak.
And when twelve acres more or less
Were added to the north,
With curious mind straightway explored
And mysteries brought forth.

Just to the west, a forest dark,
Yet, friendly to a boy;
Mulberry trees and the ripe red-haw
But added to my joy.
Goose-berry bushes and their thorns;
I counted nothing lost
When the tasty black-haws yielded to
The kiss of old Jack Frost.

The old foot-log that spanned the stream,
The water deep and still;
With fishing-pole I sat at dusk
And heard the Whippoorwill.
The catfish swam 'neath the piled up drift,
I seemed in a world apart.
Those days so full, the abundant life,
Are dear to an "old boy's" heart.

No more I'll know the old time thrill
That lives in the heart of a boy;
No more I'll roam through the mystic woods,
Know peace without alloy.
'Though well I know that life today
Is void of mysteries;
In rev'rent thankfulness I bow
To boyhood's memories.

HOWARD B. AUSTIN

47

Blessings on thee, little man,
Barefoot boy, with cheek of tan!

John Greenleaf Whittier